What is Patriarchy ?

GW00685447

Kamla Bhasin

kali for women

What is Patriarchy? was published in 1993 by

Kali for Women
B 1/8 Hauz Khas
New Delhi 110 016

First reprint, 1994
Second reprint, 1998

ISBN: 81-85107-73-4

Typeset by Vision Wordtronic Pvt.Ltd.,111/56 Nehru Place
New Delhi 110 019
Printed at Raj Press, R-3 Inderpuri
New Delhi 110 012

Introduction

Many of us involved with different programmes and activities for women's development over the years, have found it necessary to understand the system which keeps women dominated and subordinated, and to unravel its workings in order to work for women's development in a systematic way. For years I looked at women's oppression in a piecemeal fashion; the fragments began to form a pattern when I started to look at them as *part of a system* -- the system of patriarchy. It was not easy to understand, initially; not being an academic I was not trained to immediately grasp concepts and abstractions. Gradually, listening to friends who were academics, reading bits and pieces here and there, things became clearer. What really helped me was a month-long workshop on women and development that I organised in Bangladesh some years ago, with Amrita Chhachhi (of the Institute of Social Studies, the Hague) as resource person. That workshop clarified many issues and concepts, not just for me, but for most of the participants as well.

Since then (1987) I have been looking for short and simply written articles on the subject of patriarchy, which I could share with women and men activists. Most of what I had read was either too difficult to understand or too full of jargon, or it assumed prior knowledge of the subject. So I started initiating discussions on patriarchy in different workshops with the help of my notes and of Amrita's presentation at Bangladesh. During these discussions my own understanding became clearer, and I also found some articles and books which were very good. I decided to try to put all that I had read, liked and understood together in an accessible and, I hope, useful form.

In this pamphlet, I try to look at patriarchy *as we experience it in our lives and as a concept which explains women's subordination.* (Some

1

theories regarding its origin are introduced here, but very briefly. For a more detailed understanding other readings will be necessary.) It is intended for activists who may not have access to books and journals or the kind of time required to go through them all; but I hope that the writers whose work I have drawn upon will be iuuminating and will encourage at least some activists to read more on the subject. What we desperately need is more conceptual work on the nature, origin and roots of pratiarchy in South Asia so that we can understand our own situation better.

The material is presented in a question and answer style, a format that I have used earlier in a pamphlet on *Feminism*, and one that people find easy to assimilate.

What is Patriarchy ?

Q. What do we mean by patriarchy?

A. The word patriarchy literally means the rule of the father or the "patriarch", and originally it was used to describe a specific type of "male-dominated family"—the large household of the *patriarch* which included women, junior men, children, slaves and domestic servants all under the rule of this dominant male. Now it is used more generally to refer to male domination, to the power relationships by which men dominate women, and to characterise a system whereby women are kept subordinate in a number of ways. In South Asia, for example, it is called *pitrasatta* in Hindi, *pidarshahi* in Urdu and *pitratontro* in Bangla.

The subordination that we experience at a daily level, regardless of the class we might belong to, takes various forms — discrimination, disregard, insult, control, exploitation, oppression, violence — within the family, at the place of work, in society. The details may be different, but the theme is the same.

Q. How does patriarchy actually manifest itself? Can we recognise it in our own lives?

A. Anyone who has experienced even subtle discrimination, bias or non-acceptance feels and knows it, even though they may not be able to name it. Whenever women have talked about their experiences as women in workshops or trainings, they have actually described the different forms of patriarchal control that they have personally experienced. A few examples will illustrate what I mean. Each of them represents a specific form of discrimination and a particular aspect of patriarchy.

"I heard my family was unhappy when I was born. They wanted a boy." *(Son preference)*

"My brothers could demand food, they could stretch out their

3

hands and take what they wanted. We were told to wait for it to be given. We sisters and our mother had to make do with whatever was left over." *(Discrimination against girls in food distribution)*

"I have to help my mother with the household work, my brothers don't." *(Burden of household work on women and young girls)*

"It was a struggle to go to school. My father thought it was not necessary for us girls to study." *(Lack of educational opportunities for girls)*

"I could not go out to meet friends or to play."

"My brothers can come back at any time but I have to be back before dark." *(Lack of freedom and mobility for girls)*

"My father used to often beat my mother." *(Wife-battering)*

"My brothers are worse than my father. They don't want me to talk to any boys." *(Male control over women and girls)*

"Because I was not willing to give in to the demands of my boss I was thrown out of my job." *(Sexual harassment at work)*

"I have no share in my father's property. My husband's property is also not mine. Actually there is no home I can call my own." *(Lack of inheritance or property rights for women)*

"I have to submit my body to my husband whenever he wants it. I have no say. I fear sex. Don't enjoy it." *(Male control over women's bodies and sexuality)*

"I wanted my husband to use family planning methods but he refused. He also did not give me permission to get operated myself." *(No control over fertility or reproductive rights)*

As we begin to reflect on them the fragments of these experiences gradually start forming a pattern, and we realise that each one of us has had to struggle in one way or another against this discrimination. The feeling and experience of subordination destroy self-respect, self-esteem and self-confidence and set limits on our aspirations. Every courageous act we perform to assert ourselves is condemned as "unfeminine". We are called *beparda* (shameless) as soon as we try to step out of our defined spaces and roles.

Norms and practices which define us as inferior to men, which

4

impose controls on us, are present everywhere: in our families, social relations, religions, laws, schools, textbooks, media, factories, offices.

As we listen to each other we realise that this subordination is not the fate of a few of us who are unfortunate, nor is it some "vicious" men who exploit or oppress some women. We begin to understand that what we are up against is a *system*, a system of male domination and superiority, of male control, in which women are subordinate.

Q. Does the term patriarchy then sum up the kind of male domination we see around us all the time?

A. Yes, you could say so. But it is more than just a term: feminists use it like a concept, and like all other concepts it is a tool to help us understand our realities. It is defined by different people in different ways. Juliet Mitchell, a feminist psychologist, uses the word patriarchy to refer to kinship systems in which men exchange women, and to the symbolic power that fathers exercise within these systems. This power she says, is responsible for the "inferiorised" psychology of women. Sylvia Walby in her book, *Theorising Patriarchy* calls it "a system of social structures and practices in which men dominate, oppress and exploit women". As I said earlier and as Sylvia Walby reminds us, *it is important to understand patriarchy as a system* because this helps us to reject the notion of biological determinism (which says that men and women are naturally different because of their biology or bodies and are therefore assigned different roles) or the notion that *every* individual man is always in a dominant position and *every* woman in a subordinate one.

Linked to this system is the *ideology* that men are superior to women, that women are and should be controlled by men and that women are part of men's property. In some South Asian languages, for example, the words used for husband are *swami, shauhar, pati, malik,* — all words which mean "lord" or "owner".

Q. Is patriarchy the same everywhere?

A. No, not always. Its nature can be and is different in different classes in the same society; in different societies, and in different periods in history. The broad principles remain the same, i.e., men are in control, but the nature of this control may differ. For example the experience of patriarchy was not the same in our grandmothers' time as it is today; it is different for tribal women and for upper-caste

5

Hindu women; for women in the USA and women in India. Each social system or historical period throws up its own variations on how patriarchy functions, and how social and cultural practices differ. We will discuss this in detail a little later, but it is important to recognise these differences so that we can, both, analyse our own situation better and come up with appropriate strategies to deal with it.

Q. What is it that men control in a patriarchal system?

A. Normally the following areas of women's lives can be said to be under patriarchal control.

1. Women's productive or labour power
Men control women's productivity both within the household and outside, in paid work. Within the household women provide all kinds of free service to their children, husbands and other members of the family, throughout their lives. In what Sylvia Walby calls the "patriarchal mode of production", women's labour is expropriated by their husbands and others who live there. She says housewives are the producing class, while husbands are the expropriating class; their back-breaking, endless and repetitive labour is not considered work at all and housewives are seen to be dependent on their husbands.

Men also control women's labour outside the home in several ways. They force their women to sell their labour or they may prevent them from working. They may appropriate what women earn; they may selectively allow them to work intermittently. Then women are excluded from better-paid jobs, they are forced to sell their labour at very low wages; or work within the home in what is called "home-based" production, a most exploitative system.

This control over and exploitation of women's labour means that *men benefit materially from patriarchy; they derive concrete economic gains from the subordination of women.* In other words, *there is a material basis for patriarchy.*

2. Women's reproduction
Men also control women's *reproductive* power. In many societies women do not have the freedom to decide how many children they want, when to have them, whether they can use contraception, or terminate a pregnancy, etc. Apart from individual male control, male

6

dominated institutions like the church or state (i.e. religion and politics) also lay down rules regarding women's reproductive capacity. This is *institutionalised* control. For example, in the Catholic Church the male religious hierarchy decides whether men and women can use birth control methods, which methods are permissible, whether women can abort unwanted children, and so on. The continuous struggle by women for the freedom to choose when, whether and how many children to have, in practically every country in the world, is an indication of how strong this control is and how reluctant men are to relinquish it. We will discuss why this is so in the next section.

In modern times, the *patriarchal state* tries to control women's reproduction through its family planning programmes. The state decides the optimum size of the country's population and accordingly, actively encourages or discourages women to have children. In India there has been an aggressive birth control programme to limit family sizes drastically. In Malaysia, women have been urged to have several children, in order to ensure a sizeable domestic market for the country's industrial products. In Europe, where birth rates are very low, women are lured through various incentives to have more children. They are given fully-paid and very long maternity leave, opportunities for part-time jobs, childcare facilities, etc.; some countries even provide for "male maternity leave". The ideology and policies of the state also change according to the demand for labour by the economy. For example, after World War II in Germany, when labour power was required to rebuild the country, women were called upon to take up jobs and participate in nation-building. Conversely, in Britain, once the war had been won, women who had participated actively on the frontlines were told to go back home now that the men could engage in peace-time activities. The famous Baby Boom of the 1950s in the U.S. is an illustration of this, and of the state's implicit endorsement of the ideology of motherhood.

This ideology of motherhood is central to the radical feminist analysis of women's situation. According to them women are subjugated mainly because the burden of mothering and nurturing is forced on to them, *and only on them*, by patriarchal societies. Motherhood is forced by depriving young women of adequate contraceptive information; the contraceptives it does make available

7

are inconvenient, unreliable, expensive and often dangerous. Patriarchy, they assert, limits abortions and often seeks to deny them entirely, but at the same time subjects women to intense and unremitting pressure to engage in sexual relations.[1]

Further, patriarchy not only forces women to be mothers, it also determines the conditions of their motherhood. This ideology of motherhood is considered one of the bases of women's oppression because it creates feminine and masculine character types which perpetuate patriarchy; it creates and strengthens the divide between private and public, it restricts women's mobility and growth and it reproduces male dominance.

3. Control over women's sexuality

This is another very important area of women's subordination. Women are obliged to provide sexual services to their men according to their needs and desires. A whole moral and legal regime exists to restrict the expression of women's sexuality outside marriage in every society, whereas customarily, a blind eye is turned towards male promiscuity. At the other end of the spectrum men may force their wives, daughters or other women in their control into prostitution, i.e. trading their sexuality. Rape and the threat of rape is another way in which women's sexuality is dominated through an invocation of "shame" and "honour". In order to control women's sexuality their dress, behaviour and mobility are carefully monitored by familial, social, cultural and religious codes of behaviour.

A radical feminist analysis says that women under patriarchy are not only mothers, they are also sexual slaves, and patriarchal ideology typically opposes women as sexual beings to women as mothers. With the partial exception of mothers, the male culture defines women as sexual objects for male pleasure. According to it, rape may not have existed in every society but it is a defining feature of patriarchy. It sees rape as an effective political device, a political act of oppression exercised by members of a powerful class on members of a powerless class: Radical feminists also focus their attention on institutionalised prostitution, pornography and forced heterosexuality as other examples of control over women's sexuality under patriarchy.

4. Women's mobility

In order to control women's sexuality, production and reproduction, men need to control women's mobility. The imposition of parda, restrictions on leaving the domestic space, a strict separation of private and public, limits on interaction between the sexes, and so on, all control women's mobility and freedom in ways that are unique to them—that is, they are gender-specific, because men are not subjected to the same constraints.

5. Property and other economic resources
Most property and other productive resources are controlled by men and they pass from one man to another, usually from father to son. Even where women have the legal right to inherit such assets, a whole array of customary pratices, emotional pressures, social sanctions and, sometimes, plain violence, prevent them from acquiring actual control over them. In other cases, personal laws curtail their rights, rather than enhance them. In all cases, they are disadvantaged. This is amply illustrated by UN statistics: "Women do more than 60 per cent of the hours of work done in the world, but they get 10 per cent of the world's income and own one per cent of the world's property."

Q. **You earlier said that all economic, political, religious, social and cultural institutions are by and large controlled by men. Can you elaborate?**

A. An analysis of the main institutions in society shows that they are all patriarchal in nature. The family, religion, media, the law are the pillars of a patriarchal system and structure. This well-knit and deep-rooted system makes patriarchy seem invincible; *it also makes it seem natural*. Let us deal with each patriarchal institution separately.

(i) The family
The institution of the family, that basic unit of society, is probably the most patriarchal. A man is considered the head of the household; within the family he controls women's sexuality, labour or production, reproduction and mobility. There is a hierarchy in which man is superior and dominant, woman is inferior and subordinate. The family is also important for socialising the next generation in patriarchal values. It is within the family that we learn the first lessons in hierarchy, subordination, discrimination. Boys learn to assert and dominate, girls to submit, to expect unequal treatment. Again, although the extent and nature of male control may differ in different families, it is never absent.

9

According to Gerda Lerner, the family plays an important role in creating a hierarchical system and keeping order in society. She writes, "The family not merely mirrors the order in the state and educates its children to follow it, it also creates and constantly reinforces that order." [2]

(ii) Religion

Most modern religions are patriarchal, defining male authority as supreme. They present a patriarchal order as being supernaturally ordained. The feminine principle of power which existed before the evolution of institutionalised religions has been gradually weakened, godessess have been replaced by gods. All major religions have been created, interpreted and controlled by upper class and upper caste men; they have defined morality, ethics, behaviour and even law; they have laid down the duties and rights of men and women, the relationship between them. They have influenced state policy and continue to be a major force in most societies; in South Asia their power and presence are enormous. In India, for instance, inspite of the fact that it is a secular country, a person's legal identity with regard to marriage, divorce and inheritance is determined by his or her religion.

There is sufficient analysis now to show how almost every religion considers women to be inferior, impure, sinful; how they have created double standards of morality and behaviour; how religious laws often justify the use of violence against "deviant" women; how inequitous relationships are sanctioned and legitimised by recourse to "religious" creeds and fundamental tenets.

(iii) The legal system

The legal system in most countries is both patriarchal and bourgeois, i.e., it favours men and economically powerful classes. Laws pertaining to family, marriage and inheritance are very closely linked to the patriarchal control over property. In South Asia every legal system considers man the head of the household, the natural guardian of children and the primary inheritor of property. Systems of jurisprudence, the judiciary, judges and lawyers are, for the most part, patriarchal in their attitudes and in their interpretation of the law.

(iv) The economic system and economic institutions

Within a patriarchal economic system, men control the economic

10

institutions, own most property, direct economic activity, and determine the value of different productive activities. Most productive work done by women is neither recognised nor paid for; their contribution to the creation of surplus through what Maria Mies has called "shadow work" is completely discounted, and housework is not evaluated at all. Moreover, women's role as producers and rearers of children and of labour power is not considered an economic contribution at all.

(v) Political systems and institutions
Almost all political institutions in society, at all levels, are male dominated, from village councils to parliament. There are only a handful of women in political parties or organisations which decide the fate of our countries. When some women do assume important political positions (Sirimavo Bandaranaike, Indira Gandhi, Benazir Bhutto, Khaleda Zia) they do so, at least initially, because of their association with some strong male political personalities, and they function within the structures and principles laid down by men. Inspite of being the only region in the world that has had so many women heads of state, the percentage of women in parliament has never and nowhere been more than ten per cent, in South Asia.

(vi) Media
Media are very important tools in the hands of upper class, upper caste men to propagate class and gender ideology. From films and television to magazines, newspapers, radio, the portrayal of women is stereotypical and distorted. Messages about male superiority and female inferiority are repeated constantly; violence against women is rampant, especially in films. As with other sectors, women are highly under-represented in the media, professionally, and biases in reporting, coverage, advertising and messaging are still very sexist.

(vii) Educational institutions and knowledge systems
Ever since learning and education became formal and institutionalised, men have assumed control over whole areas of knowledge: philosophy, theology, law, literature, the arts, science. This male hegemony over the creation of knowledge marginalised women's knowledge and experiences, their expertise and aspirations.

In many cultures women were systematically prevented from studying the scriptures, and even today there are very few who are

11

allowed to reinterpret religious and legal texts. Gerda Lerner says, We have seen how men appropriated and then transformed the major symbols of female power: the power of the Mother Goddess and the fertility goddess. We have seen how men constructed theologies based on the counterfactual metaphor of male procreativity and redefined female existence in a narrow and sexually dependent way. We have seen, firally, how the very metaphors for gender have expressed the male as norm and the female as deviant; the male as whole and powerful, the female as unfinished, mutilated and lacking in autonomy. On the basis of such symbolic constructs... men have explained the world in their own terms and defined the important questions so as to make themselves the centre of discourse.[3]

According to some feminists, patriarchal thought and knowledge are characterised by divisions, distinctions, oppositions and dualisms. Patriarchy, they claim, opposes mind to matter, self to other, reason to emotion, and enquirer to object of enquiry. In each of these oppositions one side of the dualism is valued more than the other. Patriarchal knowledge systems are also seen to emphasise specialisation, to be narrowly compartmentalised and fragmented and unable to see the wholeness of phenomena.[4]

Male dominated knowledge and education have created and perpetuated patriarchal ideology, created what Sylvia Walby calls "a variety of gender-differentiated forms of subjectivity".[5] Men and women behave, think, aspire differently because they have been taught to think of masculinity and femininity in ways which condition difference.

Q. Don't some feminists believe that there is institutionalised violence against women in many societies?

A. Yes, they do and according to them different kinds of *violence* may be used to control and subjugate women; such violence by men may even be considered legitimate. In fact, violence against women is so pervasive that Sylvia Walby calls male violence a structure. She writes, "Male violence constitutes a further structure despite its apparently individualistic and diverse form. It is behaviour routinely experienced by women from men. Male violence is systematically condoned and legitimated by the state's refusal to intervene against it except in exceptional instances."

Violence against women was one of the first issues taken up by the international women's movement for discussion and analysis. Feminist scholarship has theorised this violence in many ways, all of which are agreed on at least one point: that it is systematic and institutionalised.

According to Mary Daly, the rulers of patriarchy (males with power) wage an increasing war against life itself. "The state of patriarchy is the state of war, in which periods of recuperation from and preparations for battle are euphemistically called 'peace'." For Daly, the custom of widow-burning in India, the Chinese ritual of foot-binding, the genital mutilation of young girls in Africa, the massacre of women as witches in "Renaissance" Europe, gynocide (female killing) under the guise of American gynaecology and psychotherapy are all examples of female hating and violence against women, practiced in different cultures of the world.[6]

In South Asia violence against women has been extensively documented and commented upon and attempts have been made to see the relationship between violence and the economic exploitation of women, violence and sexuality, violence and caste and class, etc. In a conference of autonomous women's organisations (Nari Mukti Sangharsh Sammelan) held in India in 1988, the following resolution was passed:

> Women face specific forms of violence: rape and other forms of sexual abuse, female foeticide, witch-killing, sati, dowry murders, wife-beating. Such violence and the continued sense of insecurity that is instilled in women as a result keeps them bound to the home, economically exploited and socially suppressed. In the ongoing struggles against violence in the family, society and the state, we recognize that the state is one of the main sources of violence and stands behind the violence committed by men against women in the family, the work-place and the neighbourhood. For these reasons a mass women's movement should focus on the struggles against them in the home or out of it.[7]

13

Q. Can we say that male control over all these institutions benefits them directly?

A. Generally speaking, we can. Men benefit not only in terms of greater privilege and control, but economically and materially as well. Patriarchy has a **material** basis. This is what Sylvia Walby means when she says women are the producing class and men are the expropriating class. Heidi Hartmann, a feminist scholar who sees a very close link between patriarchy and capitalism says:

> The material base upon which patriarchy rests lies most fundamentally in men's control over women's labour power. Men maintain this control by excluding women from access to some essential productive resources (in capitalist societies, for example, jobs that pay living wages) and by restricting women's sexuality. Monogamous heterosexual marriage is one relatively recent and efficient form that seems to allow men to control both these areas. Controlling women's access to resources and their sexuality, in turn, allows men to control women's labour power, both for the purpose of serving men in many personal and sexual ways and for the purpose of rearing children. The services women render men, and which exonerate men from having to perform many unpleasant tasks, occur outside as well as inside the family setting. . . The material base of patriarchy, then, does not rest solely on child bearing in the family *but on all the social structures that enable men to control women's labour.*[8]

Q. Are women completely powerless in patriarchal systems?

A. In general men hold power in all the important institutions of a patriarchal society; this however does *not* imply that women are totally powerless or totally without rights, influence and resources under patriarchy. In fact, no unequal system can continue without the participation of the oppressed, some of whom derive some benefits from it. This is true of patriarchies as well. Women have risen to power by becoming queens or prime ministers, have occasionally been in control, have wrested benefits in greater or smaller measure. But all this does not change the fact that the system is male-dominated -- women are merely accomodated in it in a variety of ways. To give a parallel, in a capitalist society workers play a very

14

important role, they may even participate in management to some extent, but this does not mean that they are in control.

Gerda Lerner makes a telling point:

> Men and women live on a stage, on which they act out their assigned roles, equal in importance. The play cannot go on without both kinds of performers. Neither of them "contributes" more or less to the whole; neither is marginal or dispensable. But the stage set is conceived, painted, defined by men. Men have written the play, have directed the show, interpreted the meanings of action. They have assigned themselves the most interesting, most heroic parts, giving women the supporting roles.

In other words the problem is not with what women *do* or *are*, it is with how they are *valued* and who has the *right to assign value* to people. It is not that women are absolutely excluded from power or prestige in patriarchy — the problem is with the framework itself, and the framework is determined by men.

Q. But women also support the rule of men. Without their cooperation patriarchy would not exist. Why do they do this ?

A. For a variety of complex reasons, some of which are familiar. We know, for example, that without the help of local soldiers, policemen, civil servants, a handful of British rulers could not have managed to rule large countries and continents. Without the tacit cooperation of slaves, slavery would not have lasted for so long. It is the same with women. They are very much part of the system, they have internalised its values, they are not free of patriarchal ideology, and as we said earlier, they obviously derive some benefits from it too. An equally complex set of relationships keeps their co-operation— or complicity as some feminists call it — active. According to Gerda Lerner :

> This cooperation is secured by a variety of means: gender indoctrination; educational deprivation; the denial to women of knowledge of their history; the dividing of women, one from the other, by defining 'respectability' and 'deviance' according to women's sexual activities; by restraints and outright coercion; by discrimination in access to economic resources and political power; and by awarding class

15

privileges to conforming women. . . a form of patriarchy best described as *paternalistic dominance.*

Women have always shared the class privileges of men of their class as long as they were under 'the protection' of a man. For women, other than those of the lower classes, the 'reciprocal agreement' went like this: in exchange for your sexual, economic, political, and intellectual subordination to men you may share the power of men of your class to exploit men and women of the lower class.[9]

In order to retain privilege, women are continually renegotiating their bargaining power, so to speak, sometimes at the cost of other women. But it is important that we look at the overall system and analyse the reasons behind this. It is true that women often treat their sons better, deprive their daughters of education, restrict their freedom, mistreat daughters-in-law and so on. All this needs to be analysed in the context of the respective power and position men and women have in the family and in society. A rural woman explained this very graphically. She said, "Men in our families are like the sun, they have light of their own (they own resources, have income, they are mobile, have the freedom to take decisions, etc.) Women are like satellites without any light of their own. They shine only if and when the sun's light touches them. This is why women have to constantly compete with each other to have a bigger share of sunlight, because without this light there is no life."

Q. Do all men benefit as men from patriarchy ?

A. The answer is yes and no. Yes, because men, whether they want to or not, enjoy certain privileges *as men.* Even working class men who are powerless vis-a-vis bourgeois men, have power over their women. In South Asia, all men enjoy greater mobility, access to resources, as men, even to basics like food and health. In other ways, as discussed earlier, social, religious, legal and cultural practices privilege them as men, and consequently, accord them more rights in practically every area.

But in another sense men are also disadvantaged by patriarchy. Like women they are pushed into stereotypes, into playing certain roles; they are expected to behave in a particular way, whether they want to or not. They too are obliged to fulfil social and other

16

obligations that require them to function in a specific way. Men who are gentle and unaggressive are harassed and mocked for being sissies; those who deal on equal terms with their wives are "henpecked". I know a man who was forever subjected to ridicule because he was training to be a Kathak dancer and was fond of sewing and knitting, all feminine activities, unfit for a "real" man.

Men, too, are denied genuine choices: they do not have the option to step out of the mainstream, relinquish the role of provider and protector. Eyebrows are raised in disbelief and contempt if a young, educated man says he "does not work", he looks after the house. "Such answers befit women, not men", he is told.

But this dehumanisation can in no way be compared to or equated with the subordination of women, for two important reasons men do not, as a whole, experience it as such, and they are not discriminated against or disabled substantially because of it.

Q. What about matriarchal societies or communities like the Nairs in Kerala?

A. Actually there is no historical evidence of the existence of matriarchy, anywhere. Sometimes people confuse *matrilineal* or *matrilocal* systems with matriarchy. What existed amongst the Nairs of Kerala was matrilineality and matrilocality. It is important to distinguish between these terms. In a matrilineal society, the lineage is traced through the mother, i.e., property passes from mothers to daughters. Such communities may also be matrilocal, i.e. the husband comes to live with the wife who continues to live in her own home. Although the position of women is much better in matrilineal and matrilocal societies, they are still not matriarchal. In a matriarchal society, women would be in a dominant position, in control of state power, religious institutions, economic production, trade, etc. Even in matriarchal societies real control is in the hands of brothers and uncles, but there is no denying the fact that the status of women in such systems is far higher than it would be otherwise.

The matrilineal, matrilocal system which existed among the Nairs of Kerala and in the north-east of India has been weakening and disappearing under the pressure of patriarchal ideology, legal systems which have displaced customary and community diversity, and the pervasiveness of "modernity", which demands uniformity. Their existence, however, proves that there can be and have been

17

different ways of organising families, inheritance, residence, labour, etc., and that there is nothing fixed or immutable about a particular order. It is, after all, man-made, not pre-ordained.

Q. Nevertheless, you seem to be implying that patriarchy has become more powerful in say the last hundred years or so. Is this so?

A. It is not easy to give a clear-cut answer to this question. It is a complex issue and cannot be generalised for all societies or communities. In some ways women have definitely gained more rights (the right to vote, to inherit, for example); more opportunities (for education, training, jobs, travel), some participation in political decision-making. There is also much greater awareness about women's oppression and the need to tackle it systematically. Women themselves have organised for change. But then there are other ways in which women seem to be worse off — the incidence of violence against them has increased sharply, their objectification by the media and the commercialisation of women's sexuality have reached alarming proportions. In India, among communities where dowry was non-existent it is now being practiced; where female infanticide was unknown, girls are being killed. The project of development and modernisation itself — which some feminists see as intrinsically patriarchal, whether communist, socialist or capitalist — seems to militate against women and marginalise them further.

In agriculture, men have gained more technical education and skills, access to credit and markets, membership in cooperatives and, as a result, acquired more control over decision-making and resources. Women continue to carry the main burden of agricultural work but with much less decision-making power or control over resources. Then, in India, the sex-ratio has been steadily declining in women's disfavour since 1921. In 1921 there were 975 women per 1000 men; in 1991 there are only 929. Globalisation of trade and the international accumulation of capital have radically altered women's role in the labour force, again often to their disadvantage.

Examining the changes in the patriarchal system in Britain, Sylvia Walby points out certain features which seem to be applicable to South Asia as well. She says:

There have been changes both in the degree and form of patriarchy in Britain. Britain has seen a movement from a

18

private to a public form of patriarchy over the last century. Private patriarchy is based upon household production as the main site of women's oppression. Public patriarchy is based principally in public sites such as employment and the state. The household does not cease to be a patriarchal structure in the public form but it is no longer the chief site. In private patriarchy expropriation of women's labour takes place primarily by individual patriarchs, in public patriarchy it is collective.

On the question of whether there has been progress or regress in women's position, she says, "Patriarchy is not a historical constant. Modifications in gender relations over the last century or so have been interpreted variously as progress, regress and involving no overall change. Liberals typically define them as progress; Marxists as regress followed by stasis, and radical feminists as embracing no significant change."[10]

The Origin of Patriarchy
Some Explanations

Q. Now that we have some clarity about patriarchy as a system, the next question that arises is obviously about its origins. Has patriarchy always existed ?

A. Some people do believe that men are born to dominate and women to be subordinate. They believe that this hierarchy has always existed and will continue, and that like other rules of nature this one too cannot be changed. There are others who challenge these beliefs and say that patriarchy is not natural, it is man-made and therefore it can be changed. It has not always existed, it had a beginning and therefore it *can* have an end. In fact for over a hundred years this debate has been going on between those who believe patriarchy is natural and universal and those who say it is *not*. Here we will briefly introduce the main theories put forward by feminists regarding the existence and origin of patriarchy; readers are encouraged to refer to other writings, as well, for a deeper understanding.

The traditionalist view of patriarchy

Traditionalists everywhere accept patriarchy as biologically determined. According to Gerda Lerner, "traditionalists, whether working within a religious or a `scientific' framework, have regarded women's subordination as universal, God-given, or natural, hence immutable... What has survived, survived because it was best; it follows that it should stay that way."[11]

She summarises the traditionalist argument in the following way: it may be offered in religious terms according to which women are subordinate to men because they were so created and consequently were assigned different roles and tasks. All known societies subscribe to such a "division of labour" which has been based on a primary biological difference between the sexes: because their biological functions are distinct, they must "naturally" have different social roles and tasks. And because these differences are natural, no one can be blamed for sexual inequality or male dominance. According to traditionalist arguments, because women produce children, their chief goal in life is to become mothers, and their chief task, child-bearing and child-rearing.

The corollary to this argument is that men, having greater physical strength, become hunters and providers — and by extension warriors — while women, because they produce children and are engaged in nurturing and mothering, require protection by men. This biological, deterministic explanation, she says, comes down, unbroken, from the stone-age to present times and it believes that man is born superior.

Explanations which consider men biologically superior and the main providers of families have however been disproved on the basis of research done on hunting and gathering societies. In all these societies, big hunt provided food for only some of the time; the main and regular food supply came through the gathering activities of women and children. Moreover, in hunter-gatherer societies there is evidence of the existence of tremendous complementarity between men and women. In South Asia even today we find that in tribal societies women command a great deal of respect, and differences in the status of men and women are much less disadvantageous to women.

Then again, if male superiority and the sexual division of labour were "natural" we would not find such vast differences in the way men and women's roles are defined in different societies. There are many traditional or primitive societies in which biological differences do not make for too much hierarchy in status and power between men and women.

Such traditionalist views were, however, not the monopoly of religious ideology. Pseudo-scientist theories have also been propagated to prove that men are superior and women inferior. Many of them argue that because women bear children and menstruate they are incapacitated and hence, disabled.

Aristotle propounded similar "theories" and called males active, females passive. For him female was "mutilated male", someone who does not have a soul. In his view the biological inferiority of women makes her inferior also in her capacities, her ability to reason and therefore her ability to make decisions. Because man is superior and woman inferior, he is born to rule and she, born to be ruled. He said

21

"the courage of man is shown in commanding, of a woman in obeying".

Several feminists have pointed out that modern psychology has also perpetuated similar views. It claims that women's biology determines their psychology and, therefore, their abilities and roles. Sigmund Freud, for example, stated that for women "anatomy is destiny". Freud's normal human was male, the female, by his definition, a deviant human being lacking a penis, whose entire psychological structure supposedly centred around the struggle to compensate for this deficiency. Popularised Freudian doctrine then became the prescriptive text for educators, social workers and the general public.

Many people have challenged all these theories of male supremacy. They have proved that there is no historical or scientific evidence for such explanations. Human beings have distanced themselves from nature, they have changed. Biology is no more their destiny. There are indeed biological differences between men and women which may even lead to some differences in their roles, but they do not have to become the basis of a sexual hierarchy in which men are dominant. The dismantling of many of these theories enables us to recognise that patriarchy is man-made; historical processes have created it.

Q. Which theories deny the universality of female subordination and explore the origin of patriarchy ?

A. For over a hundred years men and women have been trying to understand the origin of patriarchy: when and why did it start? They have asked questions like: before patriarchy was there matriarchy, in which women dominated men or was there equality between the sexes? How were different roles assigned to men and women? When did the subordination begin? It is important to ask and answer these questions not just to satisfy our curiosity about our past but because an understanding of the origins of patriarchy is essential to challenge it and envisage a society without sexual hierarchy. Strategies for change have to be based on some theoretical understanding of what needs to be changed. No single explanation of the origin of patriarchy is accepted by all. Here we will present only some of the principal theories put forward, and that, too, very briefly.

22

1. Engels' explanation of the origin of patriarchy

A very important explanation for the origin of patriarchy was given by Frederick Engels in 1884 in his book, *Origins of the Family, Private Property and the State*. Engels believed that *women's subordination began with the development of private property*, when according to him, *"the world historical defeat of the female sex"* took place. He says both the division of classes and the subordination of women developed historically. There was a time when there were no class-gender differences. He speaks of three phases of society — savagery, barbarism and civilization. In *savagery* human beings lived almost like animals, gathered food and hunted. Ancestry was through the mother, there was no marriage and no notion of private property.

Gathering and hunting continued during the phase of *barbarism* and gradually agriculture and animal husbandry were developed. Men started moving further afield to hunt, while women stayed home both to mind the children and to look after the homestead. A sexual division of labour gradually developed, but women had power, and also had control over the gens (clans or communities with a common origin). Within the gens there were no classes but there were conflicts between one gen and another.

When men started domesticating animals, they also understood the principle of impregnation. They developed weapons for bigger hunt, which were then also used in inter-group fights. Slavery developed. Gens started acquiring animals and slaves, especially female slaves. This led to more division among the sexes. Men acquired power over others and started accumulating wealth in the form of animals and slaves. *All this led to the formation of private property. Men wanted to retain power and property, and pass it on to their own children. To ensure this inheritance, mother-right was overthrown.* In order to establish the right of the father, women had to be domesticated and confined and their sexuality regulated and controlled. According to Engels it was in this period, and for these reasons, that both patriarchy and monogamy for women were established.

Because surplus was now produced in areas controlled by men, women became economically dependent. Modern civilization, according to Engels was based on restricting women to the sphere of the home in order to produce heirs to inherit property. This, he said, was the beginning of the sexual double standard in marriage.

23

According to him, with the development of the state, the monogamous family changed into the *patriarchal family* in which the wife's household labour became a "private service, the wife became a head servant, excluded from all participation in social production".

"The overthrow of the mother right was the world historical defeat of the female sex. The man took command in the home also; the woman was degraded and reduced to servitude; she became the slave of his lust and a mere instrument for the production of children."

Engels made a distinction between the bourgeois woman and working- class woman. The former, according to his analysis, does not work outside the family, she is totally dependent on her husband, she is property herself. Her only function is to produce heirs. The working class woman, on the other hand, has already broken her oppression by going into production. There is no material basis for the oppression of women among the working classes. Here the basis for male domination has been wiped out and if there are traces of women's oppression it is just a hangover of the past and will disappear once the revolution takes place. According to Engels, working-class women have to struggle with their men to overthrow private property.

Engels and other Marxists explained women's subordination only in economic terms. They argued that once private property was abolished and women joined the labour force, patriarchy would disappear. The primary contradiction for them was not between sexes but between classes. The strategy suggested for women's emancipation was their joining the labour force and joining their men in class struggle.

Other men and Marxist feminists have developed Engels' thesis further. Marxist feminists accept that class contradiction is primary and take the argument further within the Marxist framework. Several feminists have critiqued Engels' explanations; new anthropological research has shown the important role women played in the development of agriculture and in subsistence production, raising serious questions regarding his "man-the-hunter" model.

Feminists also think that Engels' emphasis on economic factors makes for an inadequate explanation of women's subordination, and disagree with his argument that there is no material basis for women's subordination in working-class families. Despite this

24

however, Gerda Lerner, assessing Engels' contribution to the understanding of patriarchy writes:

> Yet, Engels made major contributions to our understanding of women's position in society and history: *(i)* he pointed to the connection between structural changes in kinship relations and changes in the division of labour on the one hand and women's position in society on the other; *(ii)* he showed a connection between the establishment of private property, monogamous marriage and prostitution; *(iii)* he showed the connection between economic and political dominance by men and their control over female sexuality; *(iv)* by locating the world historical defeat of the female sex in the period of the formation of archaic states, based on the dominance of propertied elites, he gave the event historicity. Although he was unable to prove any of these propositions, he defined the major theoretical questions for the next hundred years.[12]

2. The radical feminist and revolutionary feminist explanations

According to the radical feminists, patriarchy *preceded* private property. They believe that the original and basic contradiction is between the sexes and not between economic classes. Radical feminists consider all women to be a class. Unlike the traditionalists however they do not believe that patriarchy is natural or that it has always existed and will continue to do so.

According to their analysis gender differences *can* be explained in terms *of the biological or psychological differences* between men and women. Shulamith Firestone says women are oppressed *because of reproduction.* She believes the basis of women's oppression does lie in women's reproductive capacity *insofar as this has been controlled by men.*

Some radical feminists say there are two systems of social classes: *(i) the economic class* system which is based on relations of *production* and *(ii)* the *sex-class* system which is based on relations of *reproduction.*[13] It is the second system that is responsible for the subordination of women. According to them the concept of patriarchy refers to this second system of classes, to the rule of women by men, based upon men's ownership and control of women's reproduc-

25

tive capacities. Because of this women have become physically and psychologically dependent on men. "The precise forms of control change according to the cultural and historical period and according to developments in the economic class system. However it is the constancy of men's power and control over women's reproductive capacities which revolutionary feminists argue constitutes the unchanging basis of patriarchy."[14] But these feminists also say that *it is not women's biology itself, but the value men place on it and the power they derive from their control over it that are oppressive.*

There are other radical feminists who see patriarchy linked not to women's biology but to *men's biology.* Susan Brownmiller says women have been subordinate because of *men's ability to rape* them.[15] She says man uses his ability to rape, to intimidate and control women. This she says has led to male dominance over women and to male supremacy. And Gerda Lerner, "Elizabeth Fischer ingeniously argued that the domestication of animals taught men their role in procreation and the practice of the forced mating of animals led men to the idea of raping women. She claimed that the brutalisation and violence connected with animal domestication led to men's sexual dominance and institutionalised aggression."[16]

Then there are feminists who see patriarchy as connected to *male psychology.* Mary O' Brien believes that it is men's psychological need to compensate for their inability to bear children which made them construct institutions of dominance. Radical feminists believe that because of their biology and/or psychology men and women belong to two separate classes. Men are the ruling class and they rule through the direct use of violence, which in time, becomes institutionalised.[17]

Radical feminists have been critiqued for accepting biological determinism as a given. If this is so then how does one change society? They have also been challenged for not exploring the connections between the sex class system and the economic class system, for treating them as autonomous. Nevertheless, they have made a considerable contribution to theorising both violence and patriarchy and presented some penetrating insights into the nature of women's subordination.

Radical feminism indeed has revealed a different reality. It has shown us a world in which men control women's bodies and force women into motherhood or sexual slavery. Radical·

26

feminism has also described how much of this occurs; it has demonstrated an interlocking system of male dominant institutions that trap women and leave them with few routes of escape; it has also explored the psychic mutilation of women imprisoned in these institutions. What radical feminism has not yet done is provide an account of the underlying causes of the patriarchal system. Why have men built these institutions and why do they maintain them.[18]

3. The socialist feminist position

Socialist feminists accept and use the basic principles of Marxism but have tried to enrich and extend it by working on areas which, they believe, were neglected by conventional Marxist theory. They try to combine the Marxist and radical feminist positions because they feel both of them have something to contribute but neither is sufficient by itself.

They do not consider patriarchy to be a universal or unchanging system because of their commitment to a historical, materialist method as well as of their own observations of variety in the sexual division of labour; socialist feminists view the struggle between women and men as changing historically with changes in modes of production.[19]

They take economic class and sex class as two contradictions in society and try to see the relationship between them. According to them patriarchy is related to the economic system, to the relations of production, but it is not *causally* related. There are many other forces which influence patriarchy; ideology for example, which has played a very important role in strengthening it. Some believe that patriarchy preceded private property, that, in fact the exploitation of women made it possible. They also believe that, just as patriarchy is not a consequence only of the development of private property so, too, it will not disappear when private property is abolished. They look at both the *relations of production* and *the relations of reproduction* in their analysis. According to them the whole area of reproduction, family and domestic labour was neglected or inadequately developed by Marxist scholars, and they have directed their attention to these.

Socialist feminists avoid not only the language of "primary" or "principal" contradiction but in general are suspicious of attempts to assert that either class or gender is causally basic to the other. They

27

see the various systems of oppression as connected inseparably with each other.[20]

Q. Can we discuss some of the different schools of thought among socialist feminists?

A. There is some difference in the emphasis and focus and also in the use of concepts. Zillah Eisenstein, a socialist feminist scholar, says that one concern is how to "formulate the problem of woman as both mother and worker, reproducer and producer". She argues that male supremacy and capitalism are the core relations which determine the oppression of women. She depicts society as comprising, "on the one hand, the capitalist labour process in which exploitation occurs, and on the other, the patriarchal sexual hierarchy, in which the woman is mother, domestic labour and consumer and in which the oppression of women occurs".[21] According to her patriarchy is not a direct outgrowth of biological differentiation; it results from the ideological and political interpretations of differentiation. This is what is meant by the social relations of reproduction or the *sex-gender system*.

> For Zillah Eisenstein these relations of reproduction are not specifically capitalist relations, but are cultural relations which are carried over from one historical period to another. While the economic organisation of society may change, patriarchy, which is located in the social relations of reproduction, provides a system of hierarchical ordering and control which has been used in various forms of social organisation, among them capitalism.[22]

One socialist feminist school of thought prefers to use the concept of *subordination of women* rather than patriarchy, which they reject as being ahistorical. Patriarchy according to them is neither universal nor an all embracing phenomenon, as different kinds of relationships have always existed between men and women in history. According to them it is not sex but *gender* which is important; sex is biological, gender is social. This group is concerned with what they call gender relations.

This school of thought has gained currency among feminist scholars and more recently among development agencies, although some feminists are of the view that the very use of concepts like

28

gender serves to de-emphasise patriarchy as an analytical as well as a struggle concept. This last they believe is critical for a synthesis of theory and practice.

Then there is the *patriarchy and capital theory* view developed, amongst others, by Heidi Hartmann. This school looks at the link between patriarchy and capitalism, and argues that patriarchy links all men to each other irrespective of their class. A woman's work benefits both capital and her husband. Hartmann defines patriarchy as a set of relations which has a material base and in which there are hierarchical relations between men and solidarity among them, which in turn enable them to dominate women. *The material base of patriarchy is men's control over women's labour power.* She says :

> As feminist socialists, we must organise a practice which addresses both the struggle against patriarchy and the struggle against capitalism. We must insist that the society we want to create is a society in which the recognition of interdependence is liberation rather than shame, in which nurturance is a universal, not an oppressive practice, and in which women do not continue to support the false as well as the concrete freedoms of men.[23]

Another important socialist feminist view has been presented by Maria Mies in a paper entitled "The Social Origins of the Sexual Division of Labour."[24] She puts forward some ideas regarding the possible reasons for and the sequence of historical developments leading to the origin of gender hierarchy or patriarchy. In this paper, she says, whatever the ideological differences between the various feminist groups, they are united in their rebellion against this hierarchical relationship between men and women, which is no longer accepted as biological destiny. Their enquiry into the social foundations of this inequality and asymmetry is the *necessary consequence of their rebellion.* Emphasising the close relationship between feminist action and theory she says :

> Women who are committed to struggle against the age old oppression and exploitation of women cannot rest content with the indifferent conclusion forwarded by many academics, i.e., that the question of origins should not be raised because we know so little about them. The search for the social origins of this relationship is part of the political

29

strategy of women's emancipation. **Without understanding the foundation and the functioning of the asymmetric relationship between men and women it is not possible to overcome it.**

Mies says that there have been biologistic biases in the earlier explanations given for sex hierarchy and they need to be thoroughly understood and discarded.

> This covert or overt biological determinism, paraphrased in Freud's statement that anatomy is destiny, is perhaps the most deep-rooted obstacle for the analysis of the causes of women's oppression and exploitation. Although women who struggle for their liberation have rejected biological determinism, they find it very difficult to establish that the unequal, hierarchical and exploitative relationship between men and women is due to social, that is, historical factors. One of our main problems is that not only the analysis as such, but also the tools of the analysis, the basic concepts and definitions, are affected — or rather infected — by biological determinism.

Mies does not ask the question: *when* did the division of labour arise between men and women but : *how* did this division of labour become a relationship of dominance and exploitation; and why did this relationship become asymmetric and hierarchical? She suggests that "we should no longer look at the sexual division of labour as a problem related to the family, but rather as a structural problem of a whole society. The hierarchical division of labour between men and women and its dynamics form an integral part of dominant production relations, i.e., class relations of a particular epoch and society and of the broader national and international divisions of labour."

She believes that if we want to find a materialist concept of women and men and their history we have to first analyse their respective interaction with nature and how, in this process, they built up their own human or social nature. She disagrees with Engels and says, "If we were to follow Engels, we would have to relegate women's interaction with nature to the sphere of evolution. (This, in fact, is being done by functionalists and behaviourists all over the world.) We would have to conclude that women have not yet entered history

30

(as defined by men) and still basically belong to the animal world. History, for Engels, begins with civilization, the exploitation of woman by man and man by man." According to Mies,

> . . . male-ness and female-ness are not biological givens, but rather the result of a long historical process. In each historic epoch male-ness and female-ness are differently defined, the definition depending on the principal mode of production in those epochs. This means that the organic differences between women and men are differently interpreted and valued, according to the dominant form of appropriation of natural matter for the satisfaction of human needs. Therefore, men and women develop a qualitatively different relationship to their own bodies. Thus in matristic societies, female-ness was interpreted as the social paradigm of all productivity, as the main active principle in the production of life. All women were defined as 'mothers'. But 'mothers' then had a different meaning. Under capitalist conditions all women are socially defined as housewives (all men as breadwinners), and motherhood has become part and parcel of this housewife-syndrome. The distinction between the earlier, matristic definition of female-ness and the modern one is that the latter has been emptied of all active, creative, productive (i.e. human) qualities.

Mies goes on to say that, because women's production of new life is linked inseparably to the production of the *means* of subsistence for it, the appropriation of their bodily nature, the fact that they produce children and milk, makes them the first providers of daily food, either as gatherers or as agriculturists. She further argues that man's objective relationship to nature is qualitatively different, because men cannot experience their own bodies as being productive in the way that women can. She suggests that male self-conception as human, i.e. as being productive, is closely linked to the invention and control of tools. "Without tools man is no MAN."

Female productivity then *is the pre-condition of* male productivity. The material dimension consists in the fact that women at all times will be the producers of new women and men, and that without this production all other forms and modes of production lose their meaning.

31

If, according to Mies, women were the first producers of life, of social production, of the first tools of production and if they were also the first to initiate social relations, why were they unable to prevent the establishment of an hierarchical and exploitative relationship between the sexes? She answers this by saying that male supremacy, far from being a consequence of men's superior economic contribution, was a result of *the development and control of destructive tools through which they controlled women, nature and other men.* According to her *women invented tools for production whereas men invented bows and arrows and spears — tools for destruction.* The significance of hunting, she argues, does not lie in its economic productivity but in the particular objective relationship that it constitutes to nature.

Mies points out that it is *not the hunting technology as such* that is responsible for the constitution of an exploitative dominance - relationship between man and nature, between man and man, and man and woman. She uses recent studies on hunting societies to show that hunters do not have an aggressive relationship to the animals they hunt. The pygmies, for example, seem to be extremely peaceful people who know neither war nor quarrels nor witchcraft. Also, their hunting expeditions are not aggressive affairs, but are accompanied by feelings of compassion for the animals they have to kill. She says that as long as hunters remained confined to their limited hunting-gathering context they did not realise the exploitative potential of their *predatory mode of production.* It was the *pastoralists* who first established patriarchal relations between men and women. Men had monopoly over arms and they now knew their generative functions as well. It was this that led to a change in their relationship to nature as well as to changes in the sexual division of labour. "For pastoral nomads, women were no longer very important as producers or gatherers of food, as is the case among hunters. They were needed as breeders of children, particularly of sons. Their productivity was reduced to their 'fertility', which was appropriated and controlled by men."

From this she concludes that

> ...it is therefore probably correct to say that the pastoral nomads were the fathers of all dominance relations, particularly that of men over women... In the last analysis we can attribute the asymmetric division of labour between women

32

and men to this predatory mode of production, or rather appropriation, which is based on the male monopoly over means of coercion, i.e. arms, and on direct violence by means of which permanent relations of exploitation and dominance between the sexes were created and maintained.

Maria Mies further argues that *the asymmetric division of labour by sex, once established by means of violence, was upheld by such institutions as the family and the state and also by means of powerful ideological systems, above all the patriarchal religions, which have defined women as part of nature which has to be controlled and dominated by man.*

To summarise, the various forms of asymmetric, hierarchical divisions of labour which developed throughout history, upto the stage where the whole world is now structured into one system of unequal division of labour under the dictates of capital accumulation, are based on the social paradigm of the predatory hunter/warrior, who, without producing himself, is able by means of arms to appropriate and subordinate other producers, their productive forces and their products.

Another feminist scholar whose work I have found very useful in understanding patriarchy is Gerda Lerner. Basically, she has argued against **single cause theories and against looking for one historical moment** when patriarchy was established. She argues that it was not one event but a process developing over a period of almost 2500 years (from approximately 3100 B.C. to 600 B.C.) and a number of factors and forces that were responsible for the establishment of male supremacy as we see it today.[25]

Gerda Lerner begins by emphasising the *importance of women's history* in women's struggle against patriarchy and for equality. She began her own search into the origins of patriarchy with the conviction that it is *historical*, as a system ; that it has a beginning in history. If that is so, it can be ended by historical process, and she has tried to understand the historical process by which it becomes established and institutionalised. She develops the following propositions:

(i)   That it was the appropriation and commodification of women's sexual and reproductive capacity by men that lies at the

33

foundation of private property; that, in fact, preceded the formation of private property and class society.

(*ii*)   That archaic states were organised around, and in the form of, patriarchy, so that from its inception, the state had an essential interest in the maintenance of the patriarchal family.

(*iii*)   That it was men's experience of dominance over the women of their own group that enabled them to institute dominance and hierarchy over other people. Thus, she says, the institutionalisation of slavery began with the enslavement of women of conquered groups.

(*iv*)   That women's sexual subordination was institutionalised in the earliest law codes and enforced by the full power of the state. Their cooperation in the system was secured by various means: force, economic dependency on the male head of the family, class privileges bestowed upon conforming and dependent women of the upper classes, and the artificially created division of women into respectable and not-respectable women.

(*v*)   That class for men was and is based on their relationship to the means of production: those who owned the means of production could dominate those who did not. For women, class is mediated through their sexual ties to a man, who then gives them access to material resources.

(*vi*)   That long after women were sexually and economically subordinated to men, they still play active and respected roles in mediating between humans and gods as priestesses, seers, diviners, and healers. This explains goddess worship in earlier times.

(*vii*)   That the dethroning of the powerful goddesses and their displacement by a dominant male god occured in most near-eastern societies after the establishment of a strong and imperialistic kingship.

(*viii*)   That the emergence of Hebrew monotheism took the form of an attack on the widespread cults of the various fertility goddesses.

(*ix*)   That the actual as well as symbolic devaluing of women in relation to the divine became one of the founding metaphors

34

of western civilization. The other founding metaphor was supplied by Aristotelian philosophy, which assumes that women are incomplete and damaged human beings of an entirely different order than men. "It is with the creation of these two metaphorical contrasts, which are built into the very foundations of the symbol systems of western civilization, that the subordination of women comes to be seen as natural, hence it becomes invisible. It is this which finally establishes patriarchy firmly as an actuality and as an ideology." [26]

Q. What about patriarchy and its origins in South Asia?

A. I am aware of some attempts being made in India to understand the origin of patriarchy, taking into account the related issues of gender, caste and class. Uma Chakravarti, in an analysis of the structural framework of Indian patriarchy, argues that caste and gender hierarchies were the organising principles of the Brahmanical social order, although they did not always exist in the form in which we see them today.[27] They evolved slowly over a considerable period of time. Basing her argument on studies of early Indian history she claims that in prehistoric cultures, women's role in production and reproduction was recognised as valuable and that in the hunting-gathering stage there was no rigid sexual division of labour. (In this her analysis is fairly close to Gerda Lerner's, discussed earlier.) According to her, in the Mesolithic period in central India women appear to have participated in the hunt in addition to the important task of gathering, the major food-procuring activity in tropical climates. Based on the study of cave paintings in central India by different historians, she says that the importance of women in the hunting-gathering economy was greatly enhanced by the importance attached to the reproductive role of women. In such a society, female sexuality was not a threat and did not have to be "managed"; on the contrary since the very survival of the community depended upon it, female reproductive power was highly valued. This she says explains the worship of female power which was located in motherhood or procreation.

This worship, however, was gradually replaced by a patriarchal ideology in the *post-class* historical society which evolved after the Aryans established control over large tracts of land and subjugated the indigenous tribes whom they obviously regarded with hostility

35

and considered racially inferior to themselves. They killed many of the men and enslaved the women of the subjugated people. Uma Chakravarti argues that the first large group of people to be enslaved in early Indian history were women (a conclusion that she shares with Gerda Lerner).

In the case of Aryan women the patriarchal family had managed to establish a certain control over women inspite of the fact that they played an active productive role in the pastoral economy.

In the course of time there was a shift to an agricultural economy. By the time of the second urbanisation (circa 600 B.C.) class and caste stratification was discernible, the Brahmana was a force to reckon with and *patriarchy was well-entrenched*. The control that men were establishing over women and the tensions inherent in such a process are indicated in references in the *Rig Veda* where the relationship between gods and goddesses is often depicted as hostile. There are references also to suggest that women must be rendered powerless by ensuring that they do not gain in strength and are obedient to men and follow them. At the same time the subjugation of certain tribes and their reduction to servility made their labour available for agricultural production. Aryan women (the women of the conquering clans) *retreated into the household and were no longer associated directly with economic production.*

Like Engels, Uma Chakravarti argues that the establishment of private property and the need to have caste purity required the subordination of women and strict control over their mobility and sexuality. The mechanism of control operated through three different devices and at three different levels. The first device was *ideology*, internalised by women as *pativrata* (wifely fidelity) "whereby women accepted and even aspired to chastity and wifely fidelity as the highest expression of their self-hood. Because it was self-imposed, the hierarchical and inegalitarian social order was reproduced by the *complicity* of upper caste women; their own subordinate status was successfully invisibilised and with it patriarchy was so firmly established as an ideology that it appeared to be natural."

The second device was *law and custom*, as prescribed by the Brahmanical social code to keep deviant women under patriarchal

36

control. The third device was *the state* itself. "If a woman's male kinsmen, who were authorised to use force, did not succeed in `restraining' her, the archaic state enforced the patriarchal norms by punishing women for `transgressions' as defined by men. Ultimately it was the *over-arching support of the early state that provided for the firm establishment of patriarchy as an actuality and not merely as an ideology.*"

Uma Chakravarti recognises the existence of differences and contradictions in the values governing women in different classes, castes and regions, but she feels "on the whole, post-caste-class Brahmanised society sanitised and circumscribed female power as mother and relocated it to reside in power born out of wifely fidelity and chastity. Wifehood, not motherhood, has been the dominant strand of mythology intended to mould feminine identity in India, and it was through such models that the sexuality of women was contained within legitimate boundaries."

This duality of perceptions (between pre-class womanhood and post-caste-class womanhood) in India continues in present-day Hindu society according to Chakravarti. The power to give birth continues to be worshipped by men and women along with notions of self-restraint and fidelity.

Like Gerda Lerner, Uma Chakravarti also believes that partiarchy has been a system of benevolent paternalism in which obedient women were accorded certain rights and privileges and security. This paternalism simultaneously made the insubordination invisible and led to their complicity in it.

> ...while they participated in the process of their own subordination because they were psychologically shaped so as to internalise the idea of their own inferiority as they did elsewhere, in India they were also socialised into believing in their own *empowerment through chastity and fidelity;* through sacrifice they saw themselves as achieving both sublimation and strength. Thus they created a *strength out of their inferiority and weakness; through a rich and imaginative mythology women were narcoticised into accepting the ideology that genuine power lies in women's ability to sacrifice, in gaining spiritual strength by denying themselves access to power, or the means to it.* Through the reiteration of cultural models in the mythology women believed that they had *different* and *distinctive* power, a higher and more spiritual power, a

37

power which would save their husbands from the worst fate and even absolve them of their sins. Working together, paternalism and cultural models of womanhood in mythology virtually *erased subordination; it was thus much easier for women to be complicit in such a structure.*

Gail Omvedt, another feminist scholar and activist who has been living and working in India for almost two decades, has studied different Indian and western theories regarding the origin of patriarchy.[28] She concludes that

1. The earliest human societies (of the paleolithic and pre-paleolithic periods) were either matrifocal bands or genderless foraging societies.

2. Kinship societies (paleolithic-neolithic) in the pre-state period were substantially egalitarian, and even after the rise of the state and patriarchal influence upon them, they continue to provide significant autonomy and access to power to women through kinship networks.

3. The rise of state-class societies, with economic inequalities, militarism, alienated religions, etc., involved the first full subordination of women which is described by feminist theorists as "patriarchy" — male control of female fertility, sexuality and labour power.

Like Gerda Lerner and Uma Chakravarti, Gail Omvedt also believes that several factors like economic participation, the role of violence and force and ideology led to the creation of patriarchy, but is optimistic in her conclusions: "Simone de Beauvoir was wrong to say that society is male. State power, class exploitation may be male, but non-state, non-class and non-gender societies are possible: they have existed and they will exist again."

At this point it is important to restate the obvious : that is, there is no one theory of patriarchy or of its origin applicable and acceptable across societies and cultures. In fact as Gail Omvedt says, the term patriarchy "operates mainly at an empiricist level. It does not really tell us what is the essence of patriarchy as a system, how it functions, how it interacts with the relations of production (of material goods) or mode of production. Is sexuality or fertility or labour the most crucial? Feminist theorists themselves differ about this."

In conclusion

Generally speaking, a large number of women's groups in South Asia seem to accept the socialist feminist position, i.e., that both patriarchy and class oppression are important, are related to, and in most cases, reinforce each other, and that women have to simultaneously challenge the system of patriarchy and class and caste domination.

In South Asia during the last three decades, women and their organisations have been challenging patriarchy in different ways; their challenges have been local, sporadic and spontaneous, as well as well-thought-out, organised and coordinated, through autonomous women's formations or in association with other social movements, political parties or trade unions. In a way, women's conceptualisation of patriarchy, their attempts to analyse it as a system and to deconstruct it are themselves a powerful challenge. The subsequent application of this analysis to action at several levels — academic, grassroots, regional and international, and in society in general — has placed the issue of women's subordination on most national agendas.

Over the last two decades or more middle and working class, rural and urban women have come together in small and large groups, in formal and informal meetings, study camps and workshops to further their own understanding of oppression and male domination.

Besides such generalised opposition to patriarchy, individual women and women's organisations have challenged different manifestations of patriarchal ideology, through the media, conferences, trainings, and actual projects on the ground for women's empowerment. They have analysed and opposed in very many ways the different forms of violence women are subjected to; they have lobbied for changes in the laws, stricter implementation of existing laws, the creation of special police cells to deal with violence against women. They have created homes for battered women, support groups for women in distress, shelters and short-stay homes.

Individual women, women's organisations and feminist scholars have challenged the patriarchal assumptions and sexist biases in the health, education and legal systems of our countries and have carried out different campaigns to make these systems more gender equitable. In almost every country in South Asia women's groups have analysed the sexist bias in the media, and examined the impact of their portrayal of women, suggested guidelines and proposed alternatives. Similarly, women's groups and feminist researchers have also studied the impact of development policies and programmes on women and have attempted to interact with national governments on policy-planning and implementation.

Notes

1   See Alison Jagger's excellent presentation of the analysis of patriarchy by different strands of feminism in her book, *Feminist Politics and Human Nature* (New Jersey : Rowman and Allanheld, 1993).

2   Gerda Lerner, *The Creation of Patriarchy* (Oxford and New York : Oxford University Press, 1986), p.217.

3   Gerda Lerner, op. cit., p.219.

4   Alison Jaggar, op. cit., p.367.

5   Sylvia Walby, *Theorising Patriarchy* (Oxford : Basil Blackwell, 1990).

6   Mary Daly, *Gyn-Ecology : The Metaethics of Radical Feminism* (Boston : Beacon Press, 1978).

7   Taken from the Report of the Nari Mukti Sangharsh Sammelan, Patna, 1988.

8   Heidi Hartmann, "The Unhappy Marriage of Marxism and Feminism : Towards a More Progressive Union", in *Capital and Class* 8, Summer.

9   Gerda Lerner, op. cit.

10 Sylvia Walby, op. cit.

11 Gerda Lerner, op. cit., p.16.

12 Ibid, p.23.

13 For instance Sheila Jeffery, "The Need for Revolutionary Feminism" quoted in Veronica Beechy, "On Patriarchy", *Feminist Review*, 3.

14 Veronica Beechy, op. cit.

15 Susan Brownmiller, *Against Our Will : Men, Women and Rape* (New York : Bantam, 1976).

16 Gerda Lerner, op. cit., p.46.

17 Jaggar, op. cit., p.160.

18 Veronica Beechy, op. cit.

19 Ibid.

20 Heidi Hartmann, op. cit.

21 This paper has been reproduced in Maria Mies, et al., *Women : the Last Colony* (Delhi : Kali for Women, 1988).

22 Gerda Lerner, op. cit.

23 Ibid., pp. 8-11.

24 Uma Chakravarti, "Conceptualising Brahmanical Patriarchy in Early India : Gender, Caste, Class and State", *Economic and Political Weekly*, Apr. 3, 1993.

25 Gail Omvedt, "Patriarchy and Matriarchy", Feminist Concepts Series, SNDT, Bombay.

KALI PRIMARIES

An introductory series on a range of issues affecting women, presented and analysed from a gender perspective. Each pamphlet discusses the issue in question, highlighting the current debates, findings and problematics in each. Written in a simple and easily accessible style, they are an extremely handy and useful resource for trainers, activists, workshop organisers, students and the general reader.

Also available in this series

Violence Against Women :
New Movements and New Theories in India
Gail Omvedt

Some Questions on Feminism and its Relevance in South Asia
Kamla Bhasin & Nighat Said Khan